I0444346

This book belongs to:

____

www.ingramcontent.com/pod-product-compliance
Lightning Source LLC
Chambersburg PA
CBHW031924240526
45464CB00022B/852
9781720147169